THE
DOMVS ROMANA

RABAT MALTA

SUZANNAH DEPASQUALE
NEVILLE JUAN CARDONA

PHOTOGRAPHY
DANIEL CILIA

HERITAGE BOOKS

in association with
HERITAGE MALTA

GLOSSARY OF USED TERMS

Amphora: A clay storage jar, typically having two handles, usually fairly large in size, plump in shape, and having a narrow mouth. It was used for liquids especially to store oil, wine, or other such liquids.

Aryballos: A round globular container used to contain perfumed oil.

Astarte: The goddess of love and war, a female deity of the ancient Near East.

Bacchante: A wild woman, devotee of the god Dionysus (Bacchus.)

Bilychnis: A double-nozzled lamp.

Bulla: A round amulet worn on the chest by children of the social elite to signify free birth. When the child came of age, the bulla was placed in the household shrine known as lararium.

Domvs: An upper class town-house usually situated within the boundaries of the city walls.

Doves of Sosos : One of the most famous and diffused motifs of antiquity. This design enjoyed a widespread success among rich and noble Romans and it was copied from the design created by a certain Sosos from Pergamon (modern day Anatolia).

Emblema: An insert, used especially for a central mosaic panel, prepared separately and inserted into a pavement.

Megarian: A type of drinking- cup made in moulds, decorated in relief, and finished in the black-glossed technique. Widespread in the Hellenistic period, this type was first recognized at Megara.

Oecus: A larger room that had a similar function to the Triclinium in the Greek world. However, in Roman architecture it became an extension of the triclinium. It was mainly used as an area for entertainment to be performed.

Oinochoe: A jug having a three-lobed spout, used for pouring wine.

Opus: Word used with various adjectives to describe craftwork techniques.

Peristyle: Open inner courtyard found in Greek and Roman houses surrounded by a colonnade. It is of Hellenistic inspiration (photo page 1).

Rython : A drinking vessel shaped in the form of a horn and usually terminating in a complex figure representing a stylized animal.

Tessellatum: Commonly used in the phrase *opus tessellatum* to distinguish floor mosaic from wall mosaic and from *opus sectile*.

Terra sigillata: A red-glossed fine type of pottery often bearing the name of the potter.

Triclinium (pl. -ia): Roman dining room found in a Roman house or in the open air. It was furnished with three couches set against the walls in a u-formation on which the Romans lay to eat.

Unguentarium: A glass bottle, core-formed closed shape having a tall cylindrical neck and an ovoid body, used to store perfume or oils.

Vermiculatum: Literally 'worm-like' commonly used to describe the technique of pictorial mosaics made with minute *tesserae* that resemble the shape of a worm.

Literary Copyright © The Authors, 2005
Editorial Copyright © Heritage Books, 2005
Photography © Daniel Cilia, 2005

First published 2005   ISBN: 99932-7-031-8

INTRODUCTION

In 1881 an important archaeological site was accidentally discovered by workers engaged in a landscaping project in Rabat. It revealed outstanding Roman remains from the ancient city of *Melite* together with evidence of our Islamic cultural heritage. Investigations conducted by A.A. Caruana, Sir Themistocles Zammit and his colleagues, Robert V. Galea, Harris Dunscombe Colt, and Louis Upton Way led to the discovery of an Islamic cemetery dating to the eleventh century AD overlying the ruins of what must have been a sumptuous Roman house belonging to the first century BC.

"The Amount of potsherds obtained from the debris was astounding: cartloads of them were disposed of after a careful examination. Most of the fragments were of ordinary domestic Roman pottery, amphorae, jugs, pots, basins etc., but debris of fine ware and of art objects was not wanting. Such were the remains of clay antefixes, figurines, lamps, masks and glass vessels." Zammit 1923: 221

Melite (Mdina) was definitely one of the main hubs on the island in antiquity, thriving during the Roman and Byzantine periods between 218 BC – 869 AD, whilst taking on a different role during the Islamic presence that seems to have been fully established at around 1048-1049 AD. This led to the inner withdrawal of the city walls and the establishment of the cemetery upon previous Roman ruins.

The extensive cemetery complex containing at least 245 burials not only provided a glimpse into our rather scantily-documented medieval past but also led to the recovery of a number of unique gravestones bearing Kufic inscriptions as well as fine glazed ceramics and a remarkable silver signet ring.

On the other hand, it also revealed a magnificent upper-class town-house boasting magnificent mosaics of Hellenistic influence and a colonnaded *peristyle*, characteristic of Greek architecture. This house seems to have originally been built during the beginning of the first century BC, but remained in use up until the second century AD.

One of the most striking discoveries were the fine polychrome mosaic floors still found *in situ* that rank amongst the finest and oldest mosaic compositions from the western Mediterranean and compare with those found in Pompeii, depicting various mythological scenes as well as decorative motifs.

The Domvs was not only embellished with mosaics and architectural remains, but also with high-quality portrait sculptures of an imperial Roman family. These portrait sculptures have been dated to the middle of the first century AD, a century after the original construction of the house. The Domvs also provided a rich array of fine Roman artefacts that used to that used to form part of the domestic belongings of a Roman family, such as fine terra sigillata tableware, perfume bottles, and other items for personal adornment.

In memory of Tancred Gouder (1935-2002)

Who dedicated his entire life to Malta's archaeological
heritage and who was instrumental in developing the
Museum of Roman Antiquities in 1980.

Signet Ring

Inv. No:	**ROM/M/31**
Material:	**Silver**
Provenance:	**Domvs Romana**
Dimensions:	**25mm Diameter**
Period:	***c*.11th C.** AD

Ornamentation of the corpse in Islamic burials is a very rare practice. In fact the only significant personal possession discovered during the excavation of the Islamic cemetery is this solid silver ring inscribed in Kufic characters. Sir Themistocles Zammit records that *'a silver ring was found on the second finger of the right hand of a skeleton laid in a well-made grave. The ring is plain with a broad face on which an inscription in Kufic characters is cut'.*

The Kufic inscription reads: *'Rabbi Allah Wahid'* – 'God alone is the Lord'.

Reference: Cardona 2002:82; Zammit's Notebook 6, 1921/24: 21; M.A.R. 1921/22: III

Tombstones

Inv. No:	**ROM/ST/300;301;302**
Material:	**Marble, Stone**
Provenance:	**Domvs Romana**
Dimensions:	**Maximum 9x115x58cm**
Period:	**c.11th C.** AD

Excavations conducted on the site by Sir Themistocles Zammit in 1920-1925 revealed an extensive cemetery complex containing at least 245 burials. During the course of investigations, a large number of fragmented tombstones, prismatic in shape and bearing Nash or Kufic inscriptions, were discovered. These tombstones that belong to a type known as *mqabriyyah* seem to have originated in Maghreb. They are mainly carved out of local Globigerina Limestone, with one exception that is carved out of marble.

This type of script that was used was normally reserved for the Koran or for monumental inscriptions, whose function became purely ornamental after the twelfth century AD. Most of the inscriptions quote from the Koran; however there are some which also record the name of the deceased, and the date of death.

Reference: Cardona 2002: 83-85

Zoomorphic spout

Inv. No:	**ROM/CR/400**
Material:	**Ceramic**
Provenance:	**Domvs Romana**
Dimensions:	**15.5x10.3 cm**
Period:	***c.*11th – 13th C.** AD

The fragment of a spouted vessel was discovered by Sir Themistocles Zammit during the excavations of the Islamic cemetery conducted in the 1920s. This zoomorphic representation of an equine monster was recovered from the topsoil above the Islamic cemetery, and probably forms part of a later deposit, during the Islamic presence on the island.

Reference: Zammit 1930: 31.

STATUE OF A DRAPED FEMALE FIGURE

Inv. No:	**ROM/ST/306**
Material:	**Marble**
Provenance:	**Unknown**
Dimensions:	**68x180 cm**
Period:	***c.*3rd C. BC – 1st C. AD**

The draped statue with surviving traces of an elaborate hairstyle and the neck adorned with heavy necklaces has been attributed to represent the goddess Astarte or Isis. The provenance of this statue is still unknown but the earliest reference dates to 1647 in the book by Giovanni Francesco Abela *Della Descrittione di Malta, Isola nel Mare Siciliano con le sue Antichità ed altre Notizie, Malta.* Abela recounts that the statue stood outside the gate of Mdina.

Reference: Abela 1647:31- 32, fig 1; Ciantar 1700, pl. ii, fig. 1; J. Houel, *Voyage des isles de Sicile, Lipari, et Malte,* iv, pl.26; Ashby 1915: 32, Fig. 3.

COINS

Inv. No:	**NUM/M/01;02**
Material:	**Copper alloy**
Provenance:	**Unknown**
Dimensions:	**Maximum *c.*3 cm**
Period:	***c.*2nd - 1st C. BC**

Several ancient coins were discovered on the site by Sir Themistocles Zammit during the excavations held between 1920 and 1925. Maltese coins of Melitaion type, second brass of Constantinus and another of Maxentius were amongst the more important recovered. The examples displayed above are:

Top Image: **Semis, Obv.** Representation of the goddess Astarte-Tanit, to the left the symbol of Tanit and to the right ΜΕΛΙΤΑΙΩΝ; Rev. Three figures, Osiris holding flail and sceptre between Isis and Nephthys, each with wings crossed in front.

Bottom Image: **Quincunx, Obv.** Representation of a helmeted female head, similar to Juno Sospita, to the right marked V beneath a large crescent; Rev. Warrior in battle advancing holding a lance and shield above a star and bearing the legend ΓΑΨΛΙΤΩΝ

Reference: Azzopardi 1993, 39-43 Notebook 8, 1924/25: 18-19.

BABY RATTLE

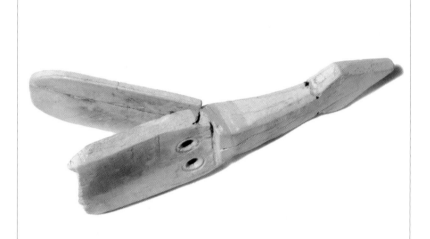

Inv. No:	**ROM/ORG/08**
Material:	**Bone**
Provenance:	**Domvs Romana**
Dimensions:	**8.5 cm, 2.75 cm**
Period:	***c*.1st C. BC**

The fragments of a tiny bone rattle seem to have been discovered from within a cave upon the site of the Domvs Romana in 1924. The cave that lies in the vicinity of the poorer houses seems to have been utilized by the inhabitants as a dumping ground for their rubbish. The rattle consisted of three parts, with two flappers attached to the body by cords being fixed through the holes.

Reference: Zammit's Notebook 7, 1922/24: 83; M.A.R. 1924/25: 4.

MASKS

Inv. No: **ROM/CR/44; ROM/CR/41**
Material: **Ceramic**
Provenance: **Unknown; Mdina**
Dimensions: **11x14 cm; 12.5x15 cm**
Period: **c.1st C. BC – 3rd C. AD**

These two terracotta masks are modelled in imitation of theatrical masks used in Greek and Roman comedy. The one to the left represents the figure known as *Egemone (il condotiero)* while that to the right represents the figure known as *Ermonio (il vecchio recalvastro)*. The latter was found at Mdina in St Paul Square and for a long time formed part of the Depiro collection. It was donated to the Museums Department in 1975 by Mrs Cassar Torregiani née Depiro.

Fragments of similar masks have also been discovered at the Domvs Romana.

Reference: Chetcuti 1997:87; Lauranta 1842: Vol VII: VLIV pgs 1-6.

Hairpins and Head of a Maenad

Hairpins:		Maenad:	
Inv. No:	**ROM/ORG/20**	*Inv. No:*	**ROM/ST/57**
Material:	**Bone**	*Material:*	**Marble**
Provenance:	**Domvs Romana**	*Provenance:*	**Unknown**
Dimensions:	**12.5 cm; 10.5 cm**	*Dimensions:*	**20x28 cm**
Period:	**2nd Century** AD	*Period:*	***c.*2nd Century** AD

The anthropomorphic pins were commonly used as hairpins by Roman women to hold their elaborate hair styles in place according to the latest fashion. They curled, braided, or pinned up their hair and kept it in position by elaborate headdresses or with plain or exquisite bronze, ivory, or bone hairpins. Numerous hairpins having spherical, segmented, or thistle shaped heads have been discovered at the Domvs Romana. The above picture illustrates the two most exquisite hairpins discovered on site.

Reference: Caruana 1881: 8; De Caro 1994: 273; MacGregor 1985: 116-122. .

The exquisitely-carved head of a Maenad, represents a bacchante votary of Bacchus who took part in his orgiastic rites, the Bacchanalia. It must have originally formed part of a larger statue, since it is broken off at the nape. Apart from distinguishing itself for its refined features it also displays an elaborate hairstyle having either an additional hairpiece or headdress.

Reference: Hall 1974: 197

Unguentarium and Balsamari

Inv. Nos:	**Various**
Material:	**Glass, bone**
Provenance:	**Unknown**
Dimensions:	**Min. *c*.2cm, , Max. *c*.14 cm**
Period:	**1st Century** AD

The Romans paid great attention to cleanliness and used various oils, perfumes, and cosmetics in their daily regime. These were considered as luxury goods and were kept in a variety of glass and bone containers known as *unguentarium*, *balsamari*, and *aryballos*. Glass rods were often used to mix and extract cosmetic substances or perfumes from the *unguentaria*. Such artefacts were often found in both domestic and funerary environments.

Reference: Guhl & Kroner 1994: 495.

Moulds

Inv. No:	**ROM/CR/98; 101**
Material:	**Ceramic**
Provenance:	**Domvs Romana**
Dimensions:	**Diameter max. 14 cm**
Period:	**1st C. BC – 2nd C. AD**

The clay moulds with their circular container were probably used as cubicles for melting metals. Several fragments of these implements were found at the Domvs Romana. They seem to indicate that they were used for the production of a particular object. The liquid metal would be placed within the circular depression with excess fluid running out to the edge via the gutter thus allowing molten metal to be poured off. These clay implements still bear evidence that they have been heated in a strong fire.

Reference: Zammit's Notebook 7, 1922/24: 28; M.A.R. 1922/23: 6.

BUCKETS

Inv. No:	**ROM/M/23**
Material:	**Copper alloy**
Provenance:	**Ta' Ġawhar Tower**
Dimensions:	**19x14 cm**
Period:	**1st C. BC – 1st C. AD**

Various buckets and pails were manufactured in copper and bronze in antiquity. The buckets usually had two small pegs on either side of the rim, to prevent the handle from falling out of the vessel. Unlike these two small buckets, the rims were usually adorned with graceful patterns. These buckets are rather unusual in that they have been recovered one within the other. This suggests that they were either put into storage or were put aside for future smelting owing to their damage.

Reference: M.A.R. 1960: 6.

Oinochoe

Inv. No:	**ROM/M/30**
Material:	**Copper alloy**
Provenance:	**Domvs Romana**
Dimensions:	**14x18 cm**
Period:	**1st C.** AD

This fine copper ewer seems to be of apparently pre-Roman origin and was discovered in a pit to the south-west of this site. Although it is covered with thick scales of oxidation, it still reveals faintly the decoration of a lions head on the handle. Numerous ewers during the Roman period were modelled on this type of decoration taken from the archaic Greek period. It became very fashionable to model copper and bronze objects on the neo-Corinthian model.

Reference: De Caro 1994: 227; Zammit's Notebook 7, 1922/24: 90; Zammit's Notebook 8, 1924/25: 9; M.A.R. 1924/25: 4.

RYTHON

Inv. No:	**ROM/GL/27**
Material:	**Glass**
Provenance:	**Unknown tomb in Rabat, Malta**
Dimensions:	**9.9x20x14.8 cm**
Period:	**1st C.** AD

The Rython is a drinking vessel shaped in the form of a horn and usually terminates in a complex figure representing a stylized animal. This vessel has been shaped in a stylized version of a snail's head. It was often modelled off complex metal prototypes and was commonly found amongst Roman tableware. The Romans used to raise the vessel to their mouths and would drink wine through the fine hole one finds at the end.

Reference: Beretta & De Pasquale 2004: 306; Caruana 1899: 54-55. Plate XXIII, 6.

GLASS AMPHORA

Inv. No:	**ROM/GL/93**
Material:	**Glass**
Provenance:	**Unknown**
Dimensions:	**21x46.4 cm**
Period:	**1st C.** AD

This glass amphora with an elongated body tapering to a pointed end is of a rare typology. Not many examples of similar glass amphorae have been discovered from the classical period in the western Mediterranean except in the area of Pompeii. Originally it probably formed part of Roman tableware and was used for the storage of wine. Jean Houel, records that this *'vase cineraire de verre'* was discovered in a catacomb. However, Caruana records that it was recovered from the ruins of a temple at St Angelo.

Reference: Beretta & De Pasquale 2004: 200 Caruana 1882: 29; Caruana 1899: 54-55. Plate XXIII; Houel 1789: 94 & Plate CCLVI.

Cup

Inv. No: **ROM/GL/19**
Material: **Glass**
Provenance: **Unknown**
Dimensions: **8x11 cm**
Period: **1st C.** AD

This exquisitely-decorated single-footed cup is surmounted by an applied decoration that separates the base from the upper section. Its fluted upper section once possessed two curled handles of which only one now survives. The once clear glass is now completely covered in iridescence and incrustations.

Reference: None

Cup and Plate

Inv. No:	**ROM/CR/37; ROM/CR/40**
Material:	**Ceramic**
Provenance:	**Unknown**
Dimensions:	**8x8cm; 16x5cm**
Period:	**1st C. AD**

The Romans loved to entertain and they developed various typologies of tableware. Food was usually cooked in crude ceramic pots and served in fine tableware. These exquisite examples are typical Roman fine ware with a glossy red-slipped surface known as Arretine ware. They are usually distinctive and standard in shape. These ceramics are usually simply or richly decorated in relief. Arretine ware usually bear a potter's name-stamp, impressed on the base, but sometimes it appears as a feature of the relief decoration.

Reference: Hayes 1997:37-64

Megarian Bowl

Inv. No:	**ROM/CR/45**
Material:	**Ceramic**
Provenance:	**Domvs Romana**
Dimensions:	**16.5x7.5 cm**
Period:	**1st C.** BC

This exquisite bowl is reconstructed from twenty-two sherds and its underside is decorated in relief. The relief depicts a lozenge frieze boundered between beaded lines. Whereas the upper section is decorated with amphorae, each between two mythological figures, the lower section is decorated with eight acanthus leaves alternating with a flower. The base is decorated with a rosette set in a ring. This bowl mimics decorated metal ware, characteristic of the Hellenistic East which continued to be made there for a while under Roman rule.

Reference: Hayes 1997: 38-40; Zammit's Notebook 6, 1921/24: 56; Zammit's Notebook 7, 1922/24: 23-24; Zammit 1923: 222; Zammit 1930: 23.

FLASK AND DRINKING VESSEL

Inv. No:	**ROM/CR/34; ROM/CR/36**
Material:	**Terra Sigillata**
Provenance:	**Unauthorized excavations in the Rabat district**
Dimensions:	**7.5x14 cm,18x23.5 cm**
Period:	**1st C. AD**

The terra sigillata drinking horn (rython) with a bulbous body terminates on one end into an upright funnel whilst on the other end it terminates in an open point. It is constructed in this manner so that its user would raise the vessel to his mouth and drink wine from the tapered end. The flask known also as the pilgrims' flask was used to contain both water or wine and was closed by a cork stopper. Sometimes the handles also served to hang the flask with cords.

Reference: Guhl & Kroner 1994: 459; Hayes 1997: 41-52: Zammit 1930: 18.

Large Water Vessel

Inv. No:	**ROM/AM/38**
Material:	**Ceramic**
Provenance:	**Domvs Romana**
Dimensions:	**88x 85 cm**
Period:	**Circa 1st BC – 3rd C. AD**

One of the large clay vessels discovered close to a well at the Domvs Romana. This type of vessel was used for the storage of liquids, namely water. Just like other ceramics these large jars often bear a large maker's stamp on the rim or shoulder.

Reference: Zammit's Notebook 7 1922/24: 86.

TOGATE FIGURE WITH BULLA

Inv. No:	**ROM/ST/303**
Material:	**Marble**
Provenance:	**Domvs Romana**
Dimensions:	**114x50x30 cm**
Period:	**1st C.** AD

This statue portrays a young boy wearing a toga and carrying a bulla round the neck. Forming part of the imperial family discovered at the Domvs Romana, it is thought to portray the adopted son of Claudius, Nero, who succeeded him to the throne in AD 54. The bulla (*etruscum aurum*) was a pendant worn on a chain or cord as an amulet to ward off evil.

Reference: Bonanno: 1992: 23; Bonanno 1994: 53.

Portrait of Claudius

Inv. No:	**ROM/ST/304**
Material:	**Marble**
Provenance:	**Domvs Romana**
Dimensions:	**34x30 cm**
Period:	**1st C.** AD

The portrait of Emperor Claudius is one fragment out of six marble sculptures to have been discovered at the Domvs Romana. It probably pertained to a group of portrait statues, representing different members of his family. It is considered to be one of the finest and most expressive portraits that exists of this emperor who reigned over the Roman Empire between AD 41 and AD 54. The discovery of these fine statues in a private house imply that the owner of this Domvs may have been a public figure.

Reference: Ashby 1915: 40; Bonanno 1992:23-24; Bonanno 1994: 52; Caruana 1881: 7

Portrait bust of Claudia Antonia

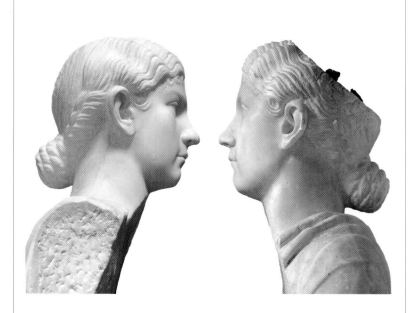

Inv. No:	**ROM/ST/305**
Material:	**Marble**
Provenance:	**Domvs Romana**
Dimensions:	**45x43 cm**
Period:	**1st C.** AD

The marble torso of a young girl wearing a distinctive hairstyle probably represents the portrait of Claudius' daughter, Claudia Antonia. Discovered at the Domvs Romana together with three other imperial statues, it may have served to represent the imperial family within this distinguished household. Such groups of portraits of the imperial dynasty occur in different places in the Roman world and were usually mounted in public locations as part of Imperial propaganda.

Reference: Ashby 1915: 39 & 41, Fig. 10; Bonanno 1992:22-23; Bonanno 1994: 52 -53; Caruana 1881: 7.

Mosaic of *Doves of Sosos* and detail

Inv. No:	*In situ*
Material:	**Marble**
Provenance:	**Domvs Romana**
Dimensions:	**71x71 cm**
Period:	**1st C. B.C**

This *emblema* in *opus vermiculatum* depicts two doves perched on a rim of a bowl. It is one of the most famous and diffused decorative motifs of antiquity, known as the *Drinking Doves of Sosos*. This design enjoyed a widespread success among the rich and noble Romans and it was copied from the design created by a renowned artist by the name of Sosos from Pergamon in the second century BC

Reference: Caselli 2002: 57; Gouder 1983: 3-4.

Mosaic of Masks

Inv. No:	**ROM/MO/01; ROM/MO/02**
Material:	**Marble**
Provenance:	**Domvs Romana**
Dimensions:	**38x100 cm, 45x72.5 cm**
Period:	**1st C. BC**

Fragments of a mosaic pavement, which originally formed part of a larger motif. This exquisite border decoration made of *opus vermiculatum* portrays a lavish garland of flowers, fruit and leaves, tied with colourful ribbon, and ornamented by theatrical masks. Similar to other festoons found in the Roman world, this mosaic flooring must have been originally decorated with eight masks. The masks probably represent personages of opposing personalities of the Greek New Comedy.

Reference: Caselli 2002: 53-54; De Caro 1994: 187; Gouder 1983: 9.

Mosaic of Oecus restoration

Inv. No:	*In situ*
Material:	**Marble**
Provenance:	**Domvs Romana**
Dimensions:	**6.3x6.4m**
Period:	**1st C.** BC

The mosaic flooring of the Oecus is constructed of two different techniques. The external bands surrounding the central frame are made of small tessarae known as *opus tessellatum*. The central mosaic is, however, made up of lozenge-shaped cut marbles and is constructed in *opus scutulatum*, giving the illusion of receding cubes. At around the first century AD the mosaic underwent some restoration and was ineptly repaired with small hexagonal terracotta tiles, marble fragments, and pottery sherds.

Reference: Gouder 1983: 4-5.

Mosaic of Bearded man

Inv. No:	*In situ*
Material:	**Marble**
Provenance:	**Domvs Romana**
Dimensions:	**6.3x4.15m**
Period:	**1st C.** BC

Detail of a mosaic floor composed of two finely-executed inner and outer polychrome frames on a plain white background. The outer frame is decorated with an elegant overlapping lyre motif, whilst that of the inner border portrays an intricate pattern of tiny triangles with a small bearded elderly face or mask of a man in one corner. It is the only partially preserved face that survived out of a total of four. Originally, this inner border must have framed a central *emblema*.

Reference: Gouder 1983: 8.

BILYCHNIS

Inv. No:	**ROM/CR/260**
Material:	**Terra cotta**
Provenance:	**Domvs Romana**
Dimensions:	**11.5x20x6 cm**
Period:	***c.*1st – 6th C.** AD

The double-spouted terracotta oil lamp is decorated with two concentric circles and the discus bears a relief of the figure of Zeus grasping a sheaf of thunderbolts and a sceptre, on an eagle. Terracotta oil lamps were commercially manufactured and were used by the Romans both in domestic and funerary environments. They were used to light up poorly-lit areas. The lamp reservoir would be filled with oil and the wick would be placed in the nozzle.

Reference: Bailey 1963: 17-23; Caruana 1899: 40-41; Guhl & Kroner, 1994: 461.

BIBLIOGRAPHY

Abela G. F. 1647, *Della Descrittione di Malta, Isola nel Mare Siciliano con le sue Antichità ed altre Notizie*. Malta.

Ashby, Thomas 1915, 'Roman Malta', *Journal of Roman Studies* 5: 1-80.

Bray, Warwick & Trump, David 1970, *The Penguin Dictionary of Archaeology*. England: Penguin Books.

Bailey, D. M 1963 *Greek and Roman Pottery Lamps*. Portsmouth: The Grosvenor Press.

Beretta, M. & De Pasquale, Giovanni 2004, *Vitrum – il vetro fra artee scienza nel mondo romano*. Ministero per I Beni e le Attivita Culturali – Soprintendenza Speciale per il Polo Museale Fiorentino. Realizzazione editoriali di Giunti Editoriali S.p.A., Firenze-Milano.

Bonanno, Anthony 1992, *Roman Malta: The Archaeological Heritage of the Maltese Islands*. Rome, World Confederation of Salesian Past Pupils of Don Bosco.

Bonanno, Anthony 1994, 'The Romans in Malta'. *Treasures of Malta*, 1/1: 48-53.

Cardona, Neville Juan 2002, 'The Saracenic cemetery on the site of the Roman Domvs, Rabat (Malta): An analysis of the archaeological evidence.' A dissertation submitted to the Department of Classics and Archaeology, Faculty of Arts in part fulfilment of a BA (Hons.) Degree in Archaeology. Malta: University of Malta.

Caselli, Antonio 2002, 'Paintings in Stone. A study on the iconographic, techniques and use of the Maltese mosaics, with reference to the development of mosaics in Hellenistic and Roman times.' A dissertation submitted to the Department of Classics and Archaeology, Faculty of Arts in part fulfilment of a BA (Hons.) Degree in Archaeology. Malta: University of Malta.

Caruana A.A. 1881, *Recent Discoveries at Notabile: a Memoir*. Malta: Government Printing Office.

Caruana A.A. 1899, *Ancient Pottery from the Ancient Pagan Tombs and Christian Cemeteries in the Islands of Malta*. Malta: Government Printing Office.

De Caro, Stefano 1994, *Il Museo Archeologico Nazionale di Napoli*. Napoli: Electa Napoli. Elemond Editori Associati: Soprintendenza Archeologica di Napoli e Caserta.

Chetcuti, Kristina 1997, 'A future for our past: Museology and Conservation in Archaeology, with special reference to the Roman town house, Rabat, Malta.' Long essay presented for the degree of BA (Hons) Archaeology, Faculty of Arts, University of Malta.

Ferrari, Daniela *et. al* 1998, *Glossario del Vetro Archeologico*, Venice.

Gouder, Tancred 1983, *The Mosaic Pavements in the Museum of Roman Antiquities at Rabat, Malta*. Malta: Government Printing Press.

Guhl, E & Kroner, W. 1994, *The Romans their life and customs*. London: Studio Editions Ltd.

Hall, James 1974, *Dictionary of Subjects and Symbols in Art*. New York: Harper & Row.

Hayes, J.W 1997, *Handbook of Mediterranean Roman Pottery*. London: British Museum Press.

Houel, Jean. 1787, *Voyage Pittoresque des Iles de Sicile , de Malte et de Lipari*, IV. Paris.

Ling, Roger 1998, *Ancient Mosaics*. London: British Museum Press.

Luaranta, Bernardo1842, *Maschere di terracotta in Real Museo di Napoli*. Napoli: Stamperia Reale. VII/VLIIV: pp. 1-6.

MacGregor, Arthur 1986, *Bone, Antler, Ivory & Horn: The technology of skeletal materials since the Roman period.* USA: Barnes and Noble.

Zammit, Themistocles

1917 'The Roman Villa Museum at Rabat' in *Archivum Melitense*, III : 1: 240-248.

1922 'Excavations in Malta'. *The Antiquaries Journal*, 2/ 2: 131-134.

1923 'Excavations at Rabat, Malta'. *The Antiquaries Journal*, 3/3: 119-225.

1930 *The "Roma Villa" Museum at Rabat – Malta*. Valletta: Empire Press.

1920 Archaeological Field-Notes, Notebook 5 (1920)

1921 Archaeological Field-Notes, Notebook 6 (1921-1922)

1922 Archaeological Field-Notes, Notebook 7 (1922-1924)

1924 Archaeological Field-Notes, Notebook 8 (1924-1925)

1920 *Report on the working of the Museum Department for the year 1920 -1921.* Malta: Government Printing Office.

1921 *Report on the working of the Museum Department for the year 1921-1922.* Malta: Government Printing Office.

1922 *Report on the working of the Museum Department for the year 1922-1923.* Malta: Government Printing Office.

1923 *Report on the working of the Museum Department for the year 1923-1924.* Malta: Government Printing Office.

1924 *Report on the working of the Museum Department for the year 1924-1925.* Malta: Government Printing Office.

1925 *Report on the working of the Museum Department for the year 1925-1926.* Malta: Government Printing Office.

1930 *Report on the working of the Museum Department for the year 1930.* Malta: Government Printing Office.

1946 *Report on the working of the Museum Department for the year 1946-1947.* Malta: Government Printing Office.

1959 *Report on the working of the Museum Department for the year 1959-1960.* Malta: Government Printing Office.

1960 *Report on the working of the Museum Department for the year 1960.* Malta: Government Printing Office.